A YEAR
Muslim
Festivals

Honor Head

WAYLAND

Explore the world with **Popcorn** – your complete first non-fiction library.

Look out for more titles in the Popcorn range. All books have the same format of simple text and striking images. Text is carefully matched to the pictures to help readers to identify and understand key vocabulary.
www.waylandbooks.co.uk/popcorn

Published in 2013 by Wayland

Wayland
338 Euston Road
London NW1 3BH

Wayland Australia
Level 17/207 Kent Street
Sydney NSW 2000

Produced for Wayland by
White-Thomson Publishing Ltd
www.wtpub.co.uk
+44 (0)843 208 7460

Editor: Jean Coppendale
Designer: Paul Cherrill
Craft artwork: Malcolm Couch
Picture researcher: Georgia Amson-Bradshaw
Islam consultant: Dr Hargey, Chairman of the Muslim Educational Centre of Oxford
Series consultant: Kate Ruttle
Design concept: Paul Cherrill

British Library Cataloging in Publication Data
Honor Head.
    Muslim festivals. -- (A year of festivals)(Popcorn)
    1. Fasts and feasts--Islam--Juvenile literature.
    I. Title II. Series
    297.3'6-dc22

ISBN: 978 0 7502 6972 8

This edition first published in 2012 by Wayland.
Reprinted in 2013
Copyright © Wayland 2012

Wayland is a division of Hachette Children's Books, an Hachette UK company.
www.hachette.co.uk

Printed and bound in China

Picture Credits: Alamy: Louise Batalla Duran Front Cover/13; Corbis: Mk Chaudhry/EPA 4; Str/Pakistan/Reuters 5; Yahya Arhab/EPA 14; Studio Dl 15; Kazuyoshi Nomachi 16; Lindsay Hebberd 18; Dreamstime: Distinctive Images 6; Getty Images: Khalil Al-Murshidi 7; Khaled Desouki 9; Peter Parks 10; Arif Ali 19; Photolibrary: Charney Magri 11; Shutterstock: Rahhal 8; Highviews 12; Sufi 17; Afaizal 20; Faraways 21

Note: When Muslims use the name of the Prophet Muhammad they usually follow it with the blessing 'Peace be upon him'. This is shown in the text here as (pbuh).

Contents

Mawlid al-Nabi

Early in the year, Muslims celebrate the birthday of the Prophet Muhammad (pbuh). Muslims believe the Prophet Muhammad (pbuh) is a messenger from God. Allah is the name of God in Arabic.

Muslim children dress up to celebrate the festival of Mawlid al-Nabi in Pakistan.

In some parts of the world, Muslims have street parades to celebrate the Prophet Muhammad's (pbuh) birthday.

Muslims are followers of the religion, Islam.

These children in Pakistan are playing music in a street parade to celebrate the birthday of the Prophet Muhammad (pbuh).

5

Lailat al-Isra wa al-Mi'raj

This festival is also called the Night Journey. Muslims remember the story of the night when the Prophet Muhammad (pbuh) went to heaven to see God.

A mother and daughter read the story of the Night Journey together.

This is an important family festival for Muslims. Children go to the mosque to pray and hear the story of the Prophet Muhammad's (pbuh) journey to heaven.

This mosque in Iraq is covered in lights to celebrate the festival.

A mosque is a special building where Muslims go to pray.

Lailat al-Qadr

Lailat al-Qadr is the time when Muslims
believe the Angel Gabriel gave the first words
of the Qur'an to the Prophet Muhammad (pbuh).

Some Muslims put the Qur'an on
a stand when they read it so that
it does not get torn or dirty.

**The Qur'an
is the holy book
of Islam. It is
written in
a language
called Arabic.**

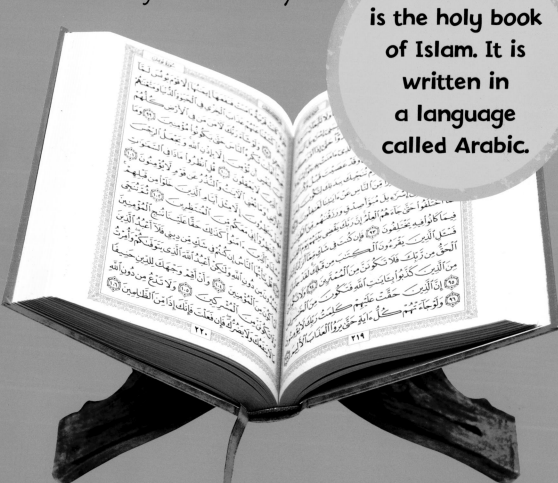

Muslims believe the Angel Gabriel first visited the Prophet Muhammad (pbuh) at night, so many Muslims stay awake during this special night.

On the night of the festival, Muslims pray and read the Qur'an.

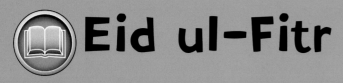# Eid ul-Fitr

Eid ul-Fitr is a time to be happy. People wear their best clothes. They go to the mosque to thank God for all the good things they have.

These Muslims in China dance and sing outside the mosque.

During this joyful festival, Muslims also remember people who do not have as much as they do. They give gifts and money to the poor.

The money Muslims give to charity is called zakat.

Eid ul-Fitr celebrates the end of Ramadan.

Eid ul-Fitr with family and friends

At Eid ul-Fitr, people who have been angry with someone forgive them. They shake hands and become friends again.

Homemade sweets are shared with friends at Eid ul-Fitr.

Many people put up special decorations in their home to celebrate this happy time. Children make cards to give to their friends and family.

Some children use henna to make beautiful patterns on their hands during Eid ul-Fitr.

Eid ul-Fitr around the world

People around the world celebrate the festival of Eid ul-Fitr in different ways. Some Muslims sing and dance to show God how thankful and happy they are.

This street market is full of sweets that are sold for Eid ul-Fitr.

In some countries, there are street parades and parties during Eid. People play musical instruments and often put on special shows.

This boy in India is celebrating the festival with sparklers.

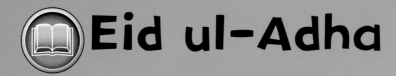Eid ul-Adha

This festival remembers the story of when God asked Abraham to sacrifice his son Ismail. This was a test to prove how much Abraham loved God. But God told Abraham to stop before Ismail was hurt.

Thousands of Muslims go on a pilgrimage to the city of Makkah in Saudi Arabia at Eid ul-Adha.

In Makkah, there is a very special place called the Ka'aba. This is a small stone building that Muslims believe was built by Abraham to worship God.

The Ka'aba is the holiest building for Muslim pilgrims. It is protected by a black cloth.

Eid ul-Adha is celebrated near the end of each year.

Muharram

Muharram is a time when Muslims remember Husayn, the grandson of the Prophet Muhammad (pbuh). Husayn was killed because of his belief in God.

Models of the mosque where Husayn was killed are carried through the streets in India.

The festival of Muharram lasts for
10 days. In some places, on the last day,
a beautiful white horse is decorated
and paraded through the streets.

The white horse is a reminder of Husayn's horse.

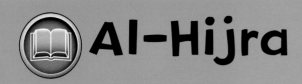 Al-Hijra

Al-Hijra is the time when Muslims think about the night the Prophet Muhammad (pbuh) escaped from his enemies. He left Makkah and went to the city of Medinah where it was safe.

Muslim pilgrims visit the Mosque of the Prophet in Medinah. The Prophet Muhammad (pbuh) is buried in this mosque.

To celebrate Al-Hijra, many countries put on huge firework displays and large parades.

These colourful fireworks are part of the festival celebrations in Turkey.

Make a mosaic place card

You will need:
- Stiff white card
- Safety scissors
- Coloured paper to make the mosaic pieces
- Glue
- Felt pen

Make some place name cards to show people where to sit for your special festival meal.

1. For each place card you will need some card about 14 cm long by 10 cm high. Fold the card in half from side to side.

14 cm

10 cm

fold

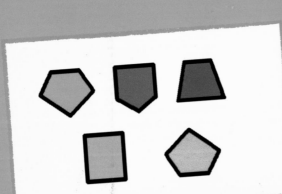

2. Cut out lots of mosaic shapes, like those shown here, from your coloured paper.

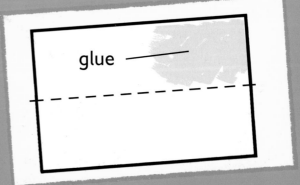

glue

3. Open out the card. Put glue on one half of the card.

4. Stick on your mosaic shapes. Leave a small white space around each shape.

5. When the mosaic is dry, fold it in half. Use a felt pen to write the person's name on the blank side.

6. Place your card on the table where the person is sitting. The name side should face the chair and the mosaic side is the table decoration.

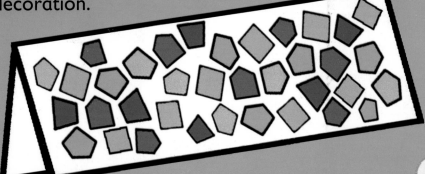

Glossary

Abraham a prophet. He is also known as Ibrahim

Angel Gabriel an angel from God. The angel passed on messages from God to the Prophet Muhammad (pbuh).

mosque a special building where Muslims meet to pray and worship God

mubarak means 'blessed' in Arabic and is a type of greeting

pilgrimage a special journey to an important holy place

prophet a messenger who passes on the word of God to the people

Ramadan the month when all Muslims fast between sunrise and sunset

Index

QUIET
TENT

For all the children at Crayke CE Primary School;
may you all be blessed with the gift of friendship. And for Mrs Sheppard,
my friend, who won this dedication for you all at an auction raising money
for refugees   A.B.

To Rob and my family, all my love   A.P.

Published by Lion Children's Books
an imprint of
Lion Hudson plc
Wilkinson House, Jordan Hill Road,
Oxford OX2 8DR, England
www.lionhudson.com/lionchildrens

Hardback ISBN 978 0 7459 7707 2
Paperback ISBN 978 0 7459 7706 5

First edition 2017

A catalogue record for this book is available from the British Library

Printed and bound in Malaysia, January 2017, LH18

Anne Booth ★ Amy Proud

I want a
Friend

LION
CHILDREN'S

"I want a friend," said Arthur,
"I want a friend *right now*.
I want to make one RIGHT AWAY
But I am not sure how."

"I want a friend," said Arthur,
"I want a friend TODAY.

I'm running fast to catch one —

But they don't want to stay."

"I'm thinking hard," says Arthur,
"I've got to make a trap.
I'm going out to catch a friend,
I need my thinking cap."

"I'll dig a hole," says Arthur,
"So when they run about,
They'll tumble in
And then I'll go
And pull my new friend out."

"That didn't work," says Arthur,
"I need another plan.
I need to make another one
As quickly as I can."

"I know the thing," says Arthur,
"I'll just rush off and get
The perfect thing to catch a friend –
A **great ginormous net**."

"That didn't work," said Arthur,
Climbing down the tree,
"How can I get a friend to stay –
Not be upset with me?"

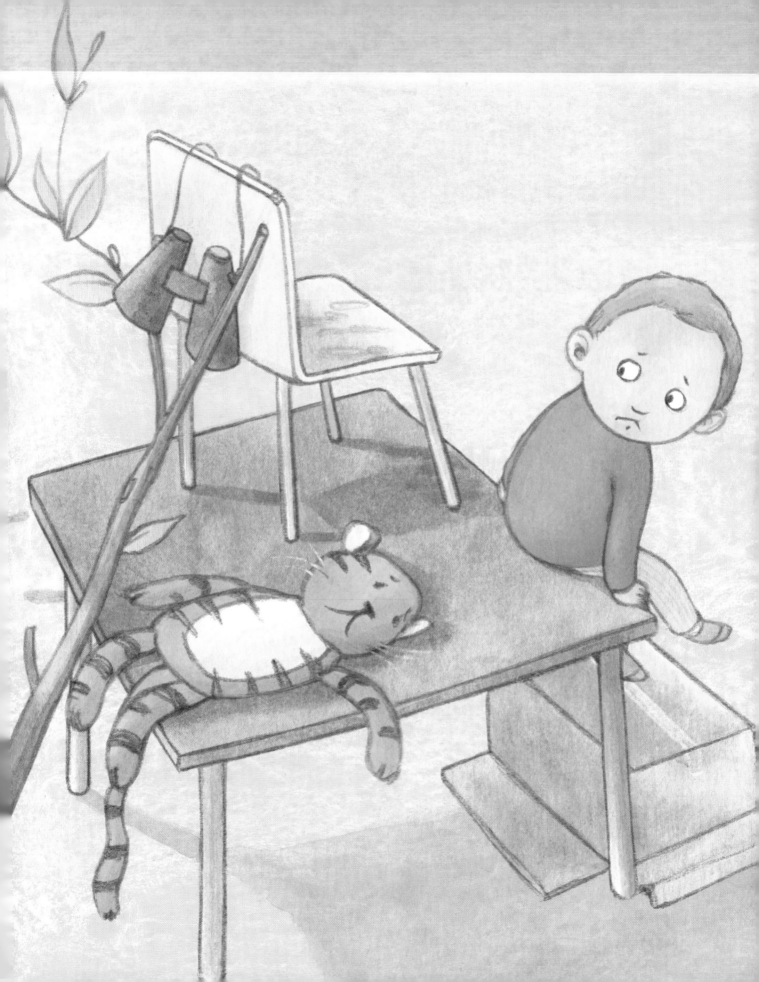

"I'm all alone," says Arthur,

"I'm feeling very sad.

All that I wanted was a friend

And now I feel so bad."

"Oh, please don't cry," says Lily,
"What would you like to play?
I'll be your friend and cheer you up,
We'll have a lovely day."

"Oh, can we race?" says Arthur.
"Yes," Lily says, **"Let's go!**

We'll both hold hands and run around
And then we'll do a show."

"Shall we dress up?" says Lily.
"I think I'll be a cat
And you can be a dragon boy –
Do you think you'd like that?"

"Oh yes! Yes, please," says Arthur
And gives a dragon roar.

"Ow!" Lily says, "That's much too loud
And made my ears feel sore."

"I'm very sorry," Arthur says,
"Please will you be my friend?"

"Of course!" says Lily, hugging him,
"*Forever with no end.*"

"I want a friend," says Martha,
"I want a friend *right now*.
I want to make one RIGHT AWAY."

Now, can we tell her how?

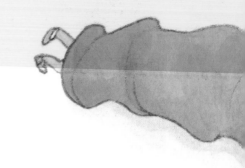